ANIMAL SUPERSTARS

WOLVERINE
POWERFUL PREDATOR

PAIGE V. POLINSKY
CONSULTING EDITOR, DIANE CRAIG, M.A./READING SPECIALIST

Super Sandcastle

An Imprint of Abdo Publishing
abdopublishing.com

abdopublishing.com

Published by Abdo Publishing, a division of ABDO, PO Box 398166, Minneapolis, Minnesota 55439. Copyright © 2017 by Abdo Consulting Group, Inc. International copyrights reserved in all countries. No part of this book may be reproduced in any form without written permission from the publisher. Super SandCastle™ is a trademark and logo of Abdo Publishing.

Printed in the United States of America, North Mankato, Minnesota
062016
092016

Editor: Rebecca Felix
Content Developer: Nancy Tuminelly, Mighty Media, Inc.
Cover and Interior Design and Production: Christa Schneider, Mighty Media, Inc.
Photo Credits: Alamy; AP Images; iStockphoto; Mighty Media, Inc.; Sergey Gorshkov/Minden Pictures; Shutterstock; SuperStock

Library of Congress Cataloging-in-Publication Data

Names: Polinsky, Paige V., author.
Title: Wolverine : powerful predator / by Paige V. Polinsky.
Description: Minneapolis, Minnesota : Abdo Pub., [2017] | Series: Animal
   superstars
Identifiers: LCCN 2016006322 (print) | LCCN 2016007038 (ebook) | ISBN
   9781680781519 (print) | ISBN 9781680775945 (ebook)
Subjects: LCSH: Wolverine--Juvenile literature.
Classification: LCC QL737.C25 P65 2016 (print) | LCC QL737.C25 (ebook) | DDC
   599.76/6--dc23
LC record available at http://lccn.loc.gov/2016006322

Super SandCastle™ books are created by a team of professional educators, reading specialists, and content developers around five essential components— phonemic awareness, phonics, vocabulary, text comprehension, and fluency—to assist young readers as they develop reading skills and strategies and increase their general knowledge. All books are written, reviewed, and leveled for guided reading, early reading intervention, and Accelerated Reader™ programs for use in shared, guided, and independent reading and writing activities to support a balanced approach to literacy instruction.

CONTENTS

WILD WEASELS

Wolverines are in the weasel family. They are big for weasels. Adults can be 44 inches (112 cm) long. They weigh up to 40 pounds (18 kg).

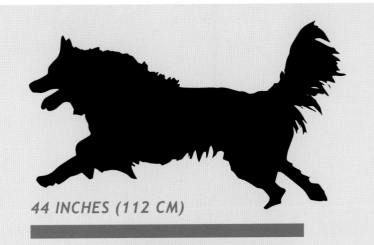

44 INCHES (112 CM)

A WOLVERINE CAN BE AS LONG AS A MEDIUM-SIZED DOG.

GREEDY EATERS

Wolverines eat anything they can find. This includes plants and **carrion**. Wolverines' sharp teeth can rip frozen meat. Wolverines also hunt.

NO WASTE

WOLVERINES EAT THEIR ENTIRE PREY. THIS INCLUDES BONES AND TEETH!

HUGE GAME

Wolverines are small. But they hunt huge game! This includes moose and **caribou**. Wolverines jump on large prey from trees.

FAST FEET

WOLVERINES CAN RUN 30 MILES PER HOUR (48 KMH).

FEARLESS FIGHTERS

Wolverines are fierce. They will fight for food. One wolverine can scare off a pack of wolves!

WHEN **DESPERATE**, WOLVERINES WILL STEAL FOOD FROM BEARS.

WIDE RANGE

Wolverines live in North America. They also live in Europe and Asia. They make dens under large stones and in snow. They mark territories. Each territory can cover hundreds of miles.

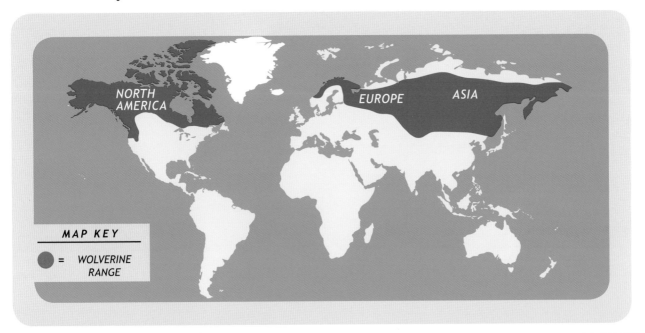

NORTH AMERICA
EUROPE
ASIA

MAP KEY

● = WOLVERINE RANGE

*WOLVERINES LIVE IN **TUNDRA** AND FORESTS.*

TOUGH TRAVELERS

Wolverines travel very far. Some roam 15 miles (24 km) a day. They will climb mountains looking for food.

HIGH CLIMB

ONE WOLVERINE CLIMBED NEARLY 5,000 FEET (1,520 M) UP A MOUNTAIN IN 90 MINUTES!

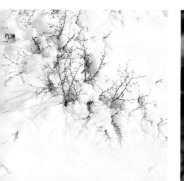

WINTER WARRIORS

Wolverines are made for cold weather. Their fur is **waterproof**. It keeps them warm. Their large paws act as snowshoes.

FAMILY TIES

Adult wolverines live alone. But they still have family bonds. **Kits** stay with their mothers for several months or up to two years. Their fathers visit them.

FUR TROUBLE

People hunt wolverines. They use wolverine fur to make clothing. Wolverines are not **endangered**. But they could be in the **future**.

A COAT HOOD LINED WITH WOLVERINE FUR

WOLVERINE SUPERSTAR

Can you imagine a wolverine superstar? What would it look like? What **awards** would it win?

WHAT DO YOU KNOW ABOUT
WOLVERINES?

1. Wolverines are in the weasel family.

True or false?

2. Wolverines have sharp teeth.

True or false?

3. Wolverine hunt moose.

True or false?

4. Wolverines live in hot desert regions.

True or false?

GLOSSARY

AWARD - a prize.

CARIBOU - a large, North American reindeer.

CARRION - flesh of dead animals.

DESPERATE - suffering extreme need or anxiety.

ENDANGERED - having few of a type of plant or animal left in the world.

FUTURE - coming or happening at a later time.

KIT - a young fur-bearing animal.

TUNDRA - a large area of flat land in northern parts of the world where there are no trees and the ground is always frozen.

WATERPROOF - made to keep water out.